[First Act]

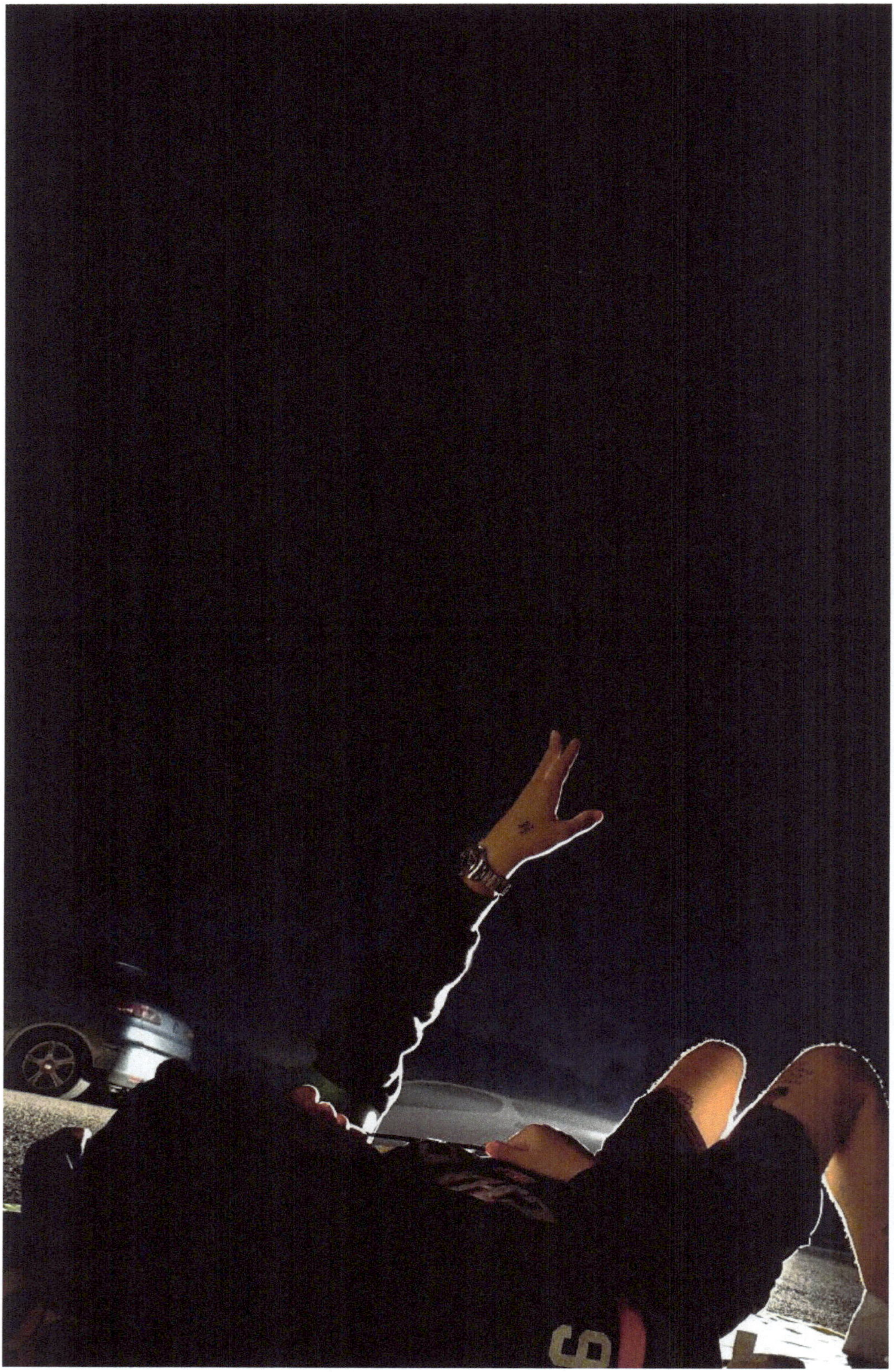

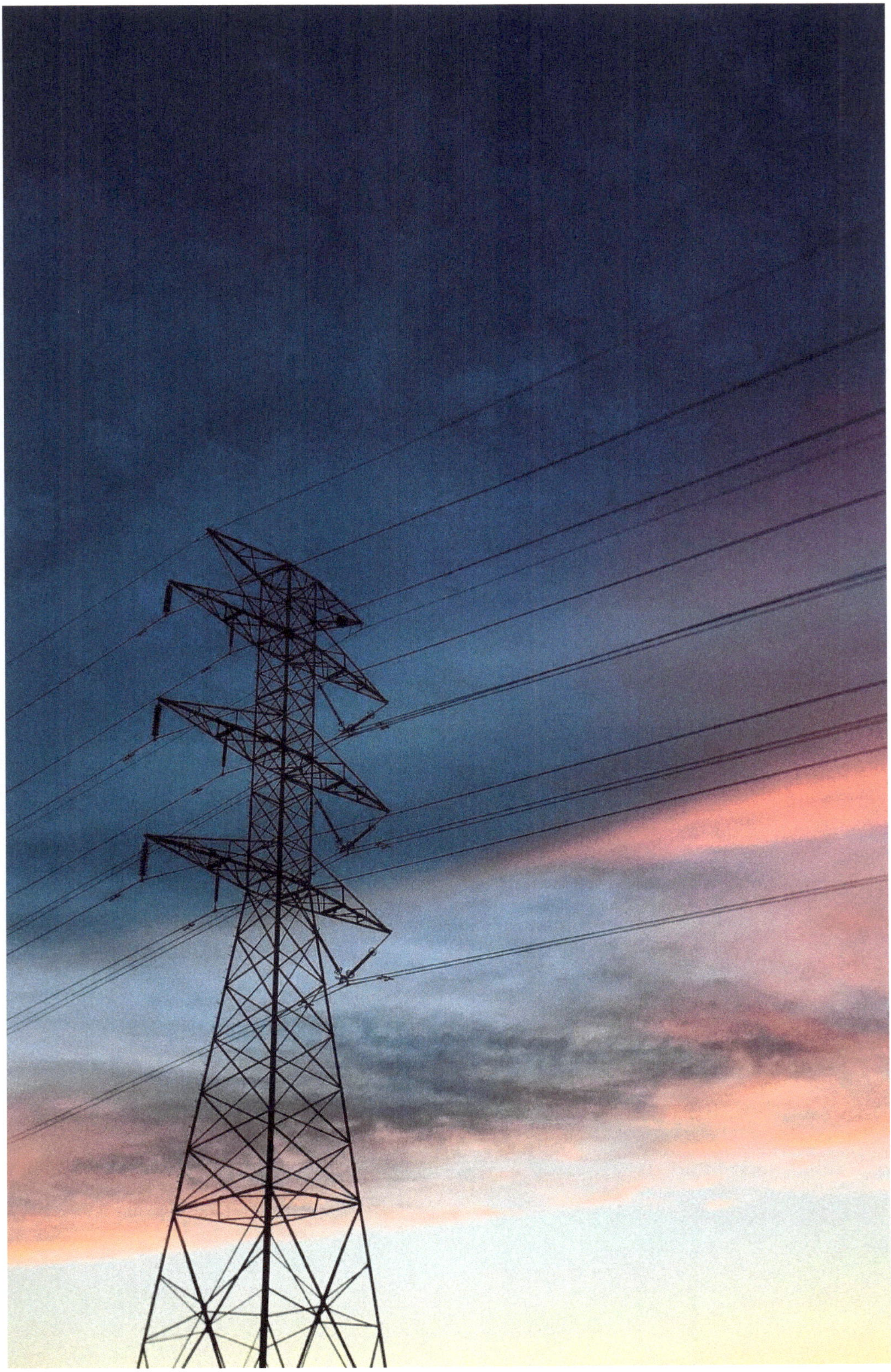

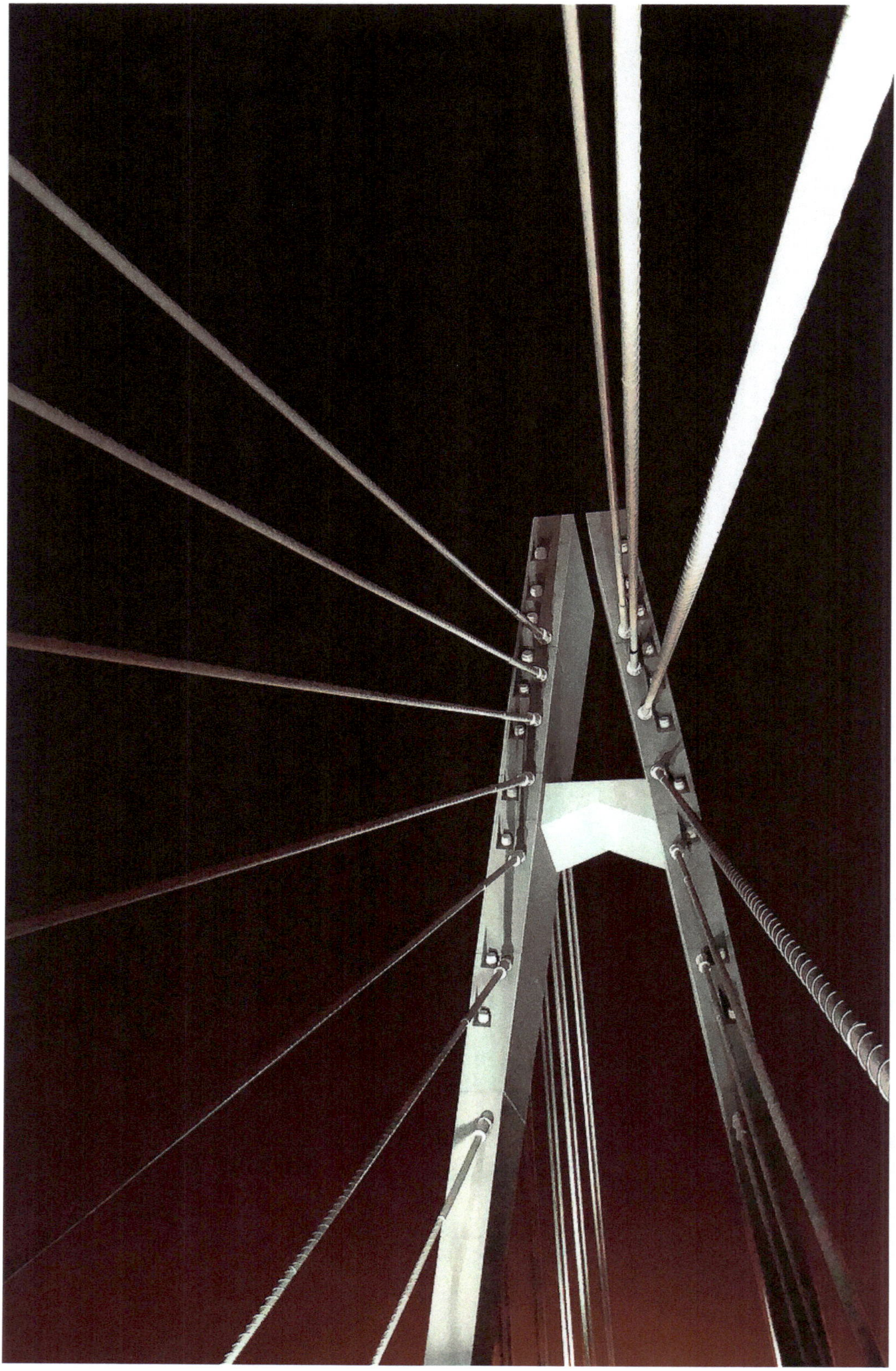

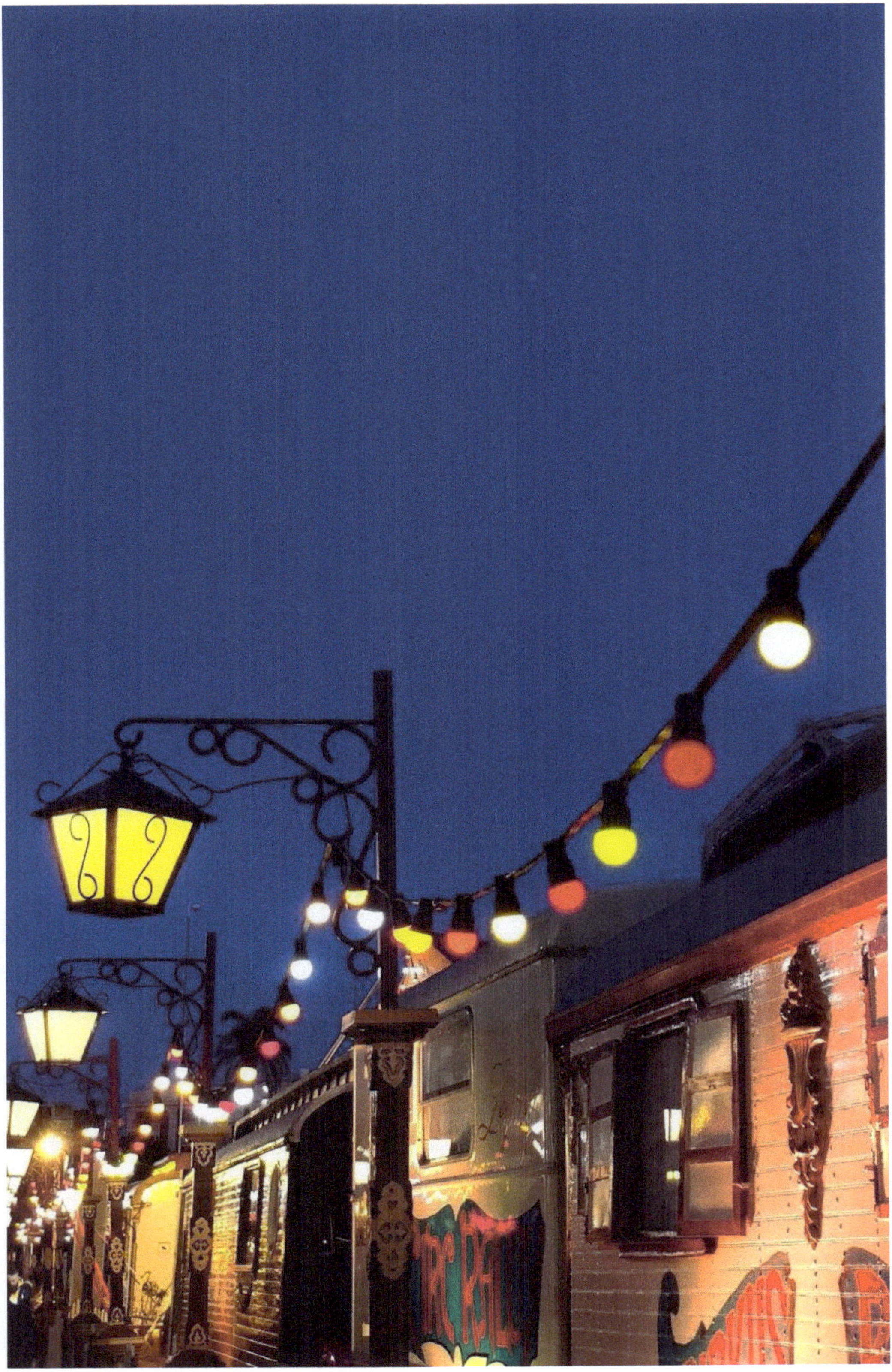

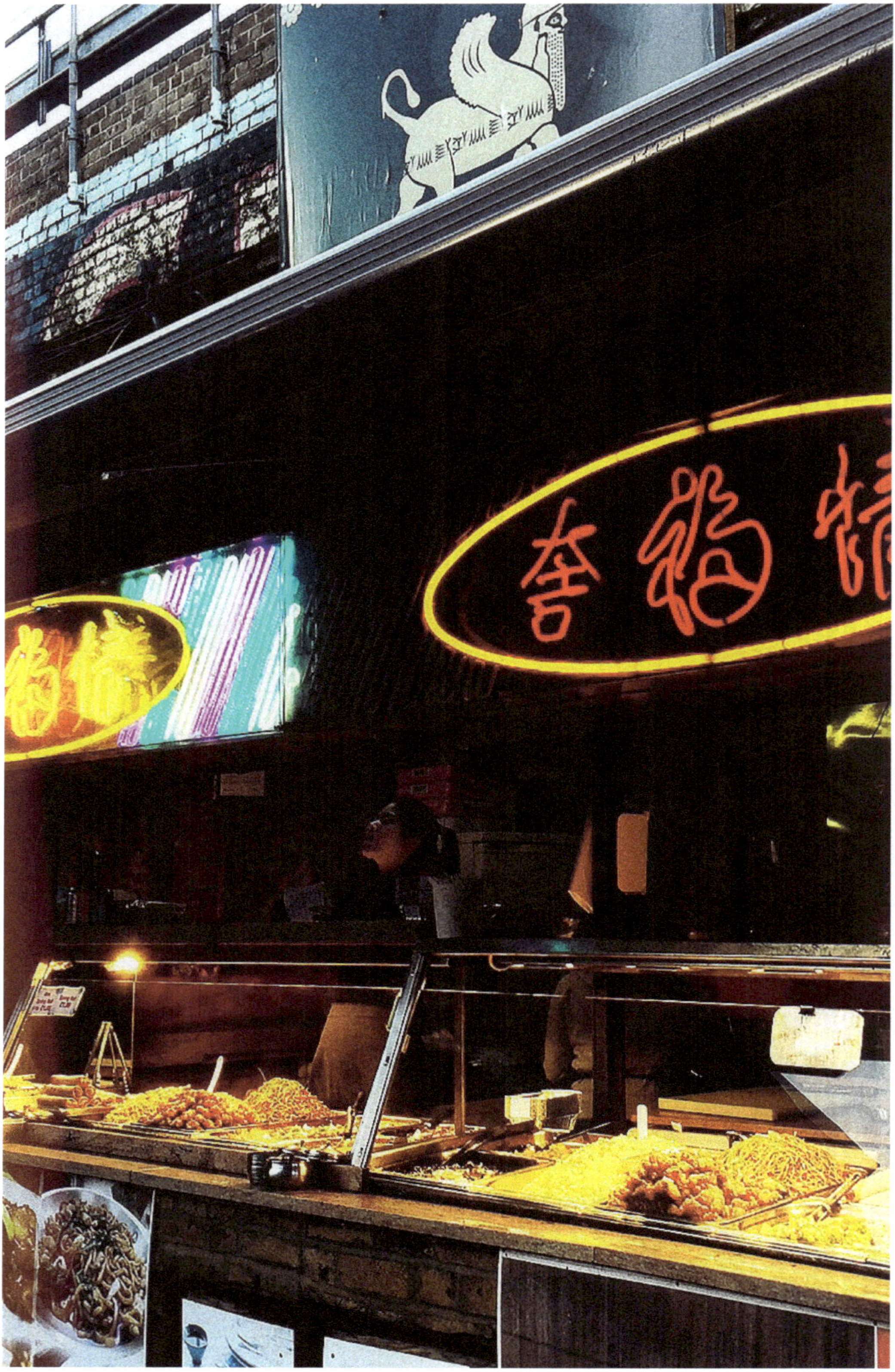

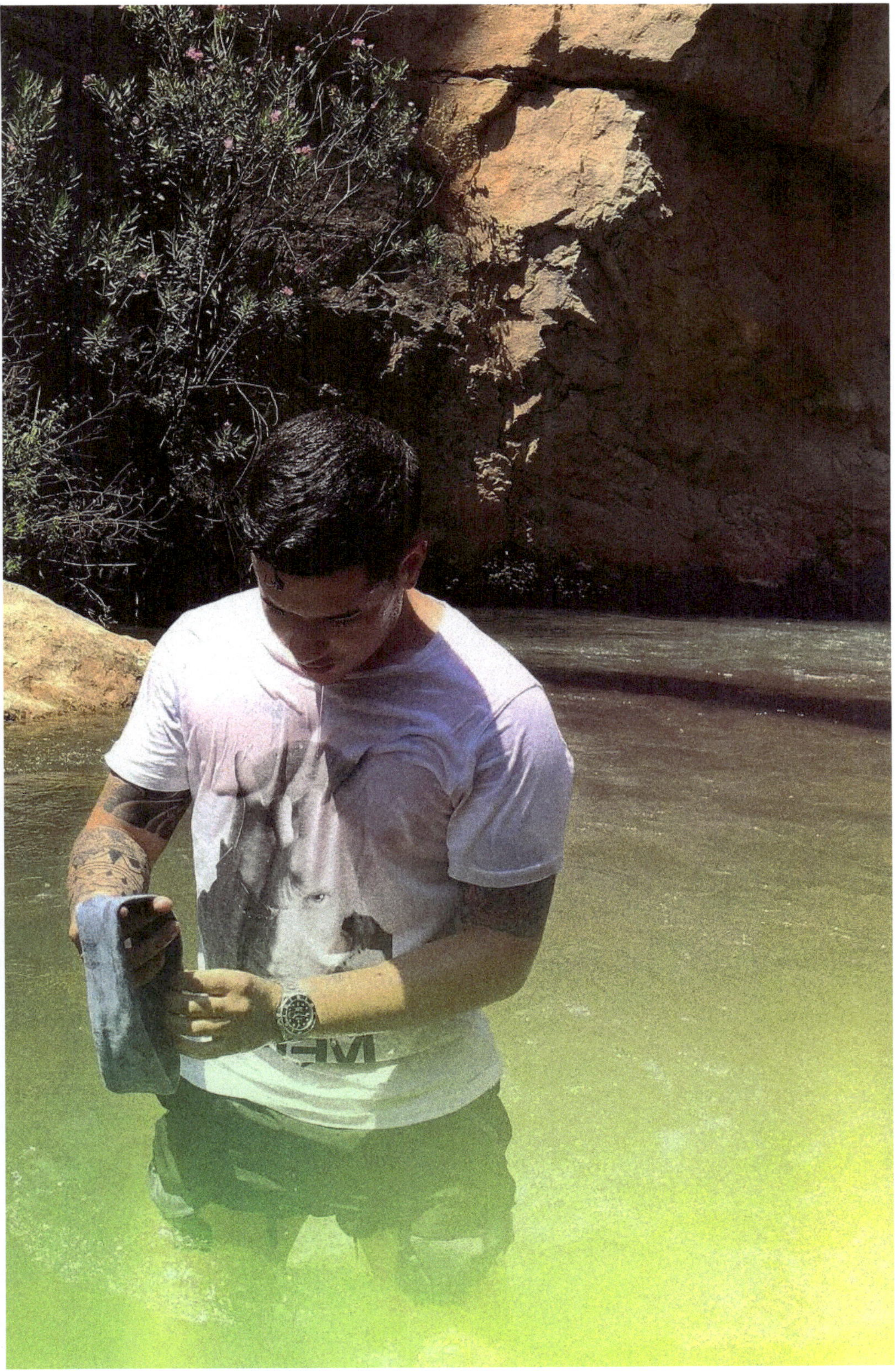

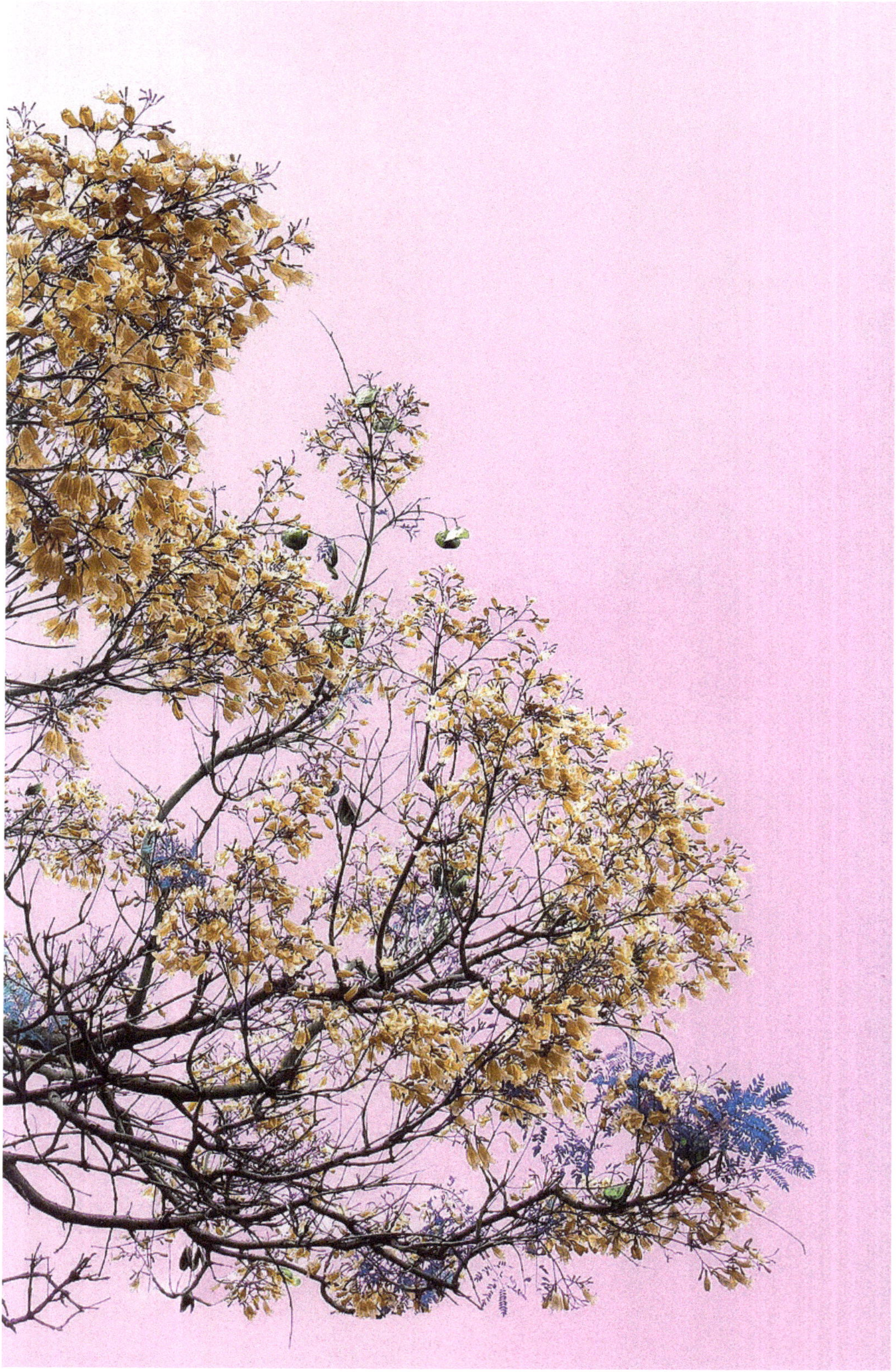

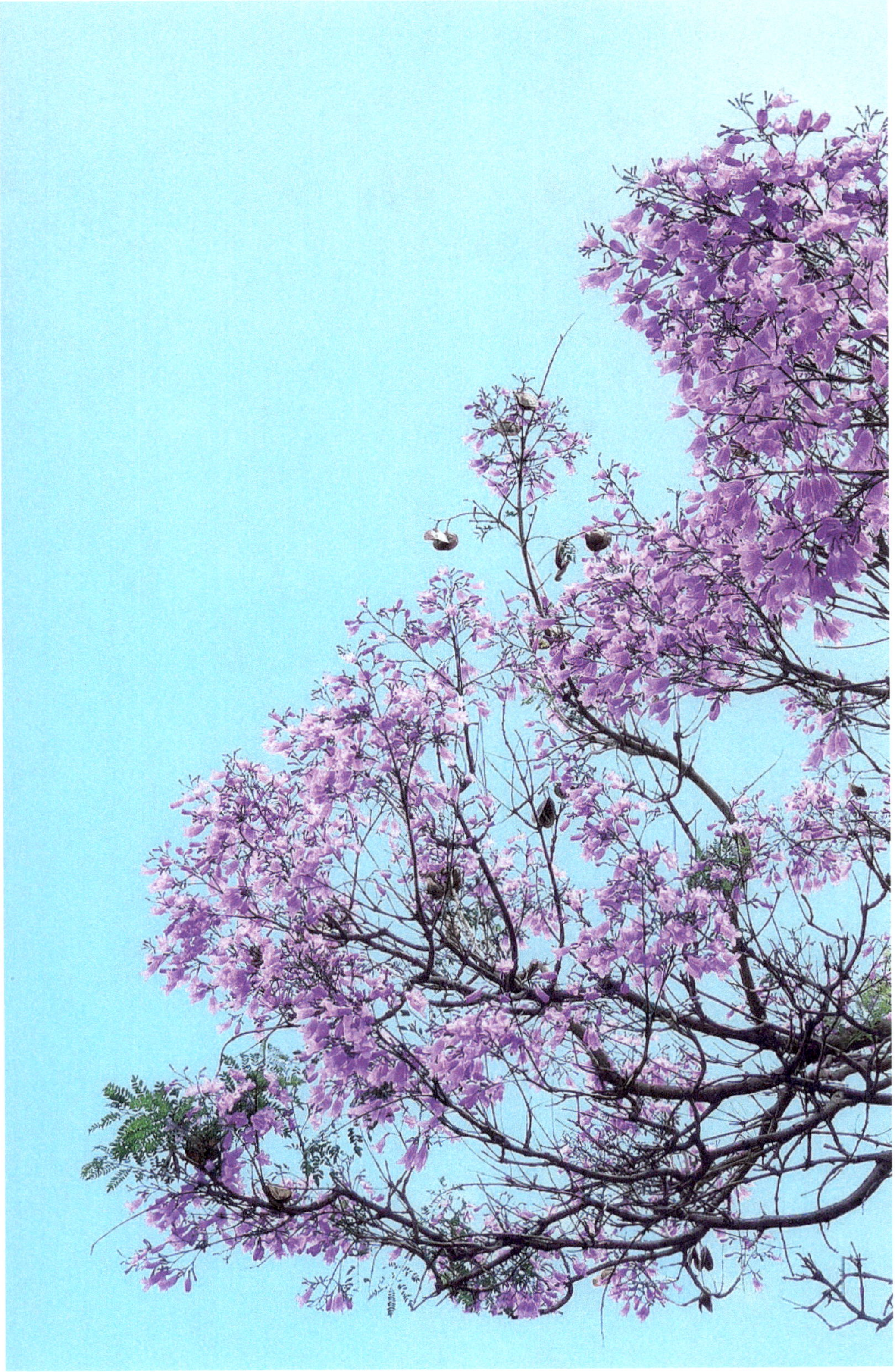

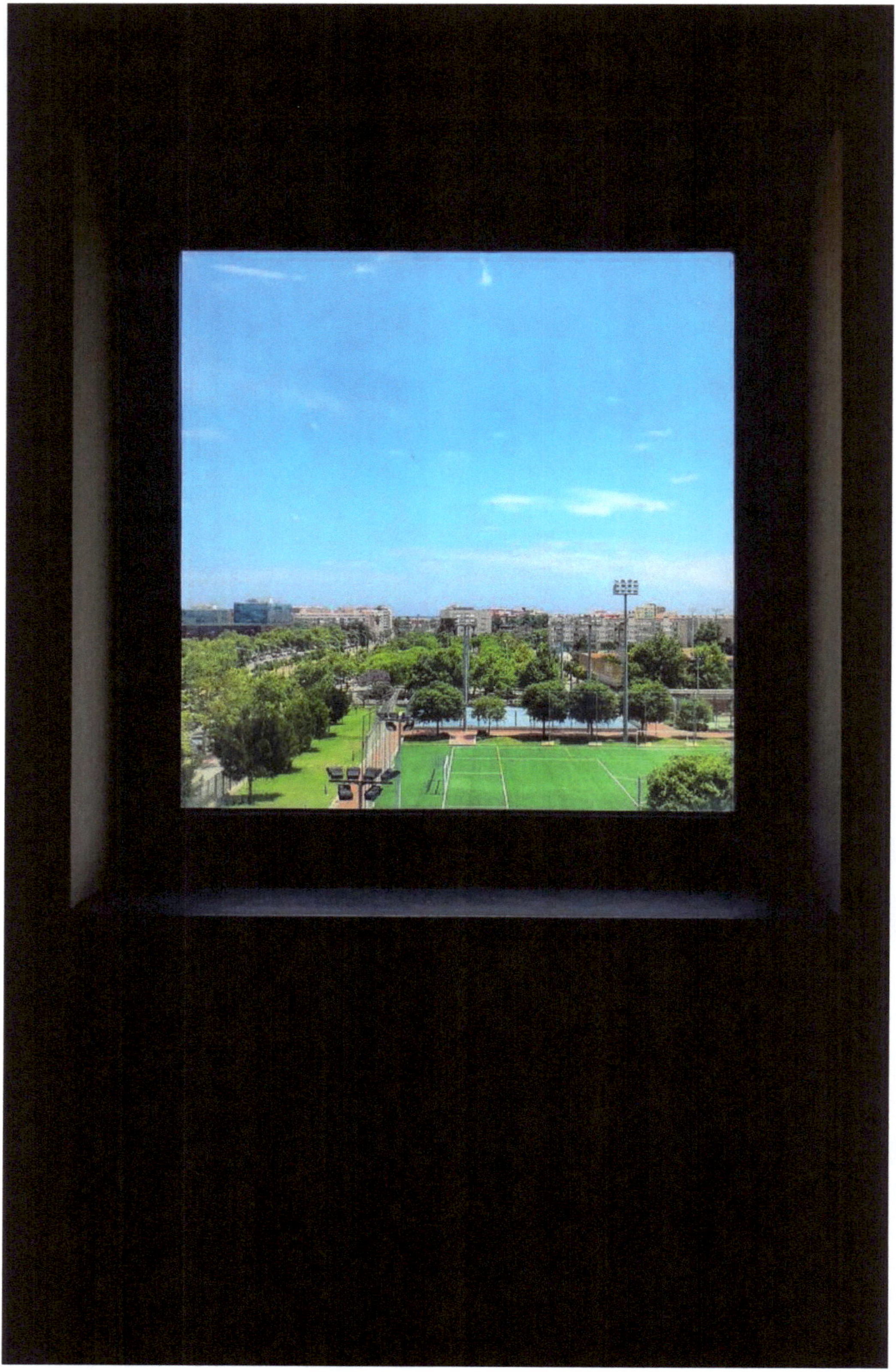

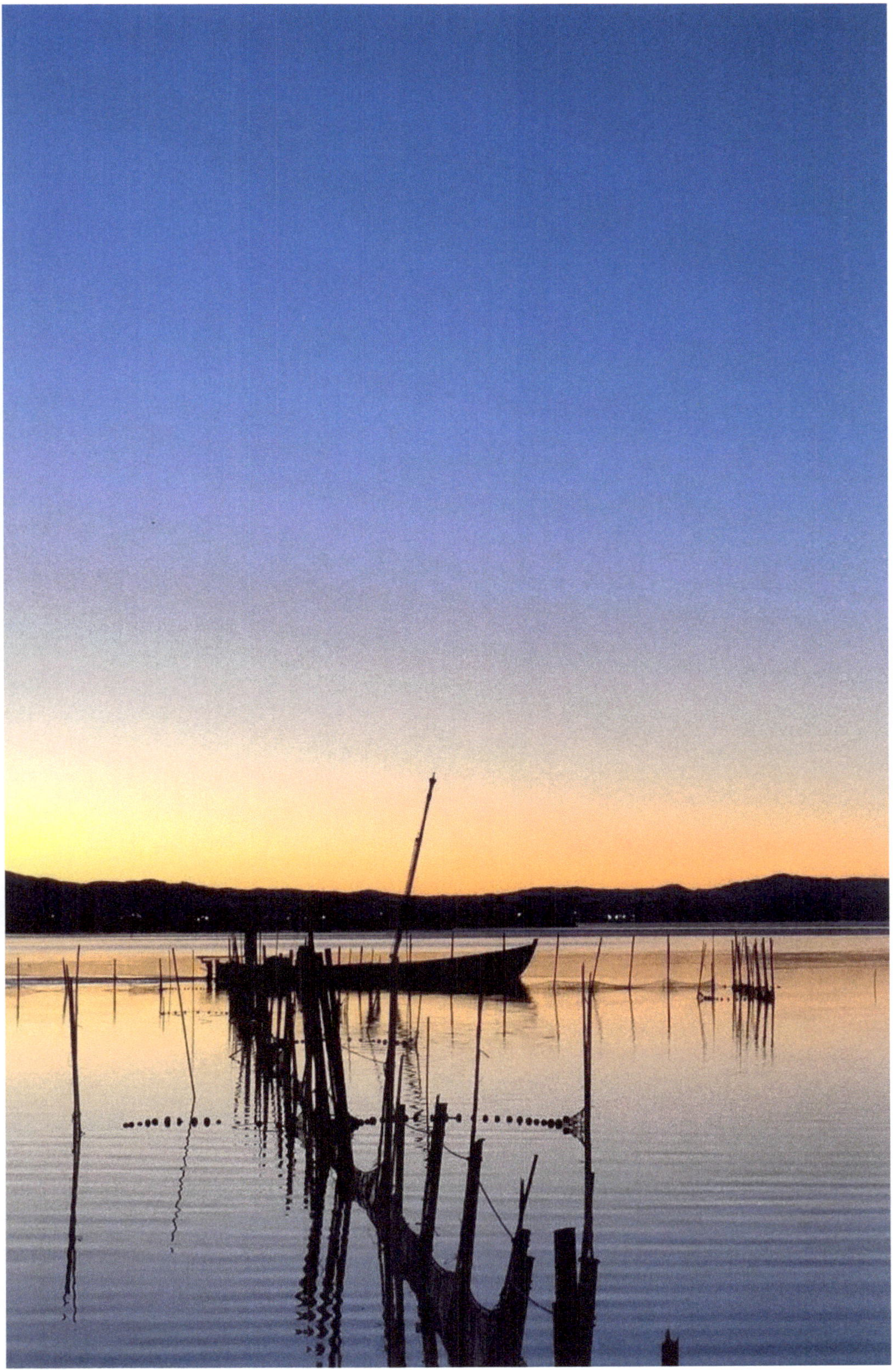

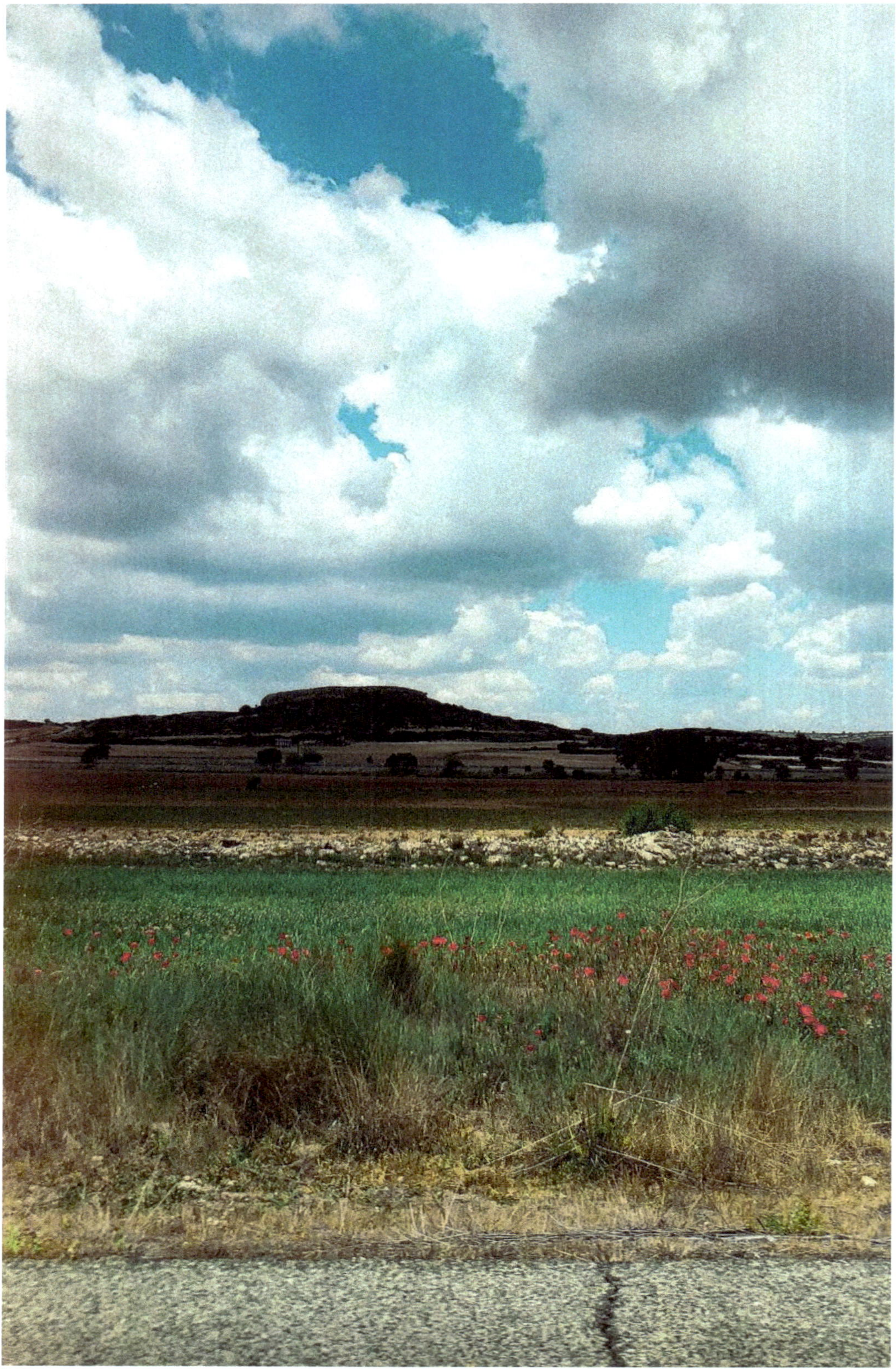

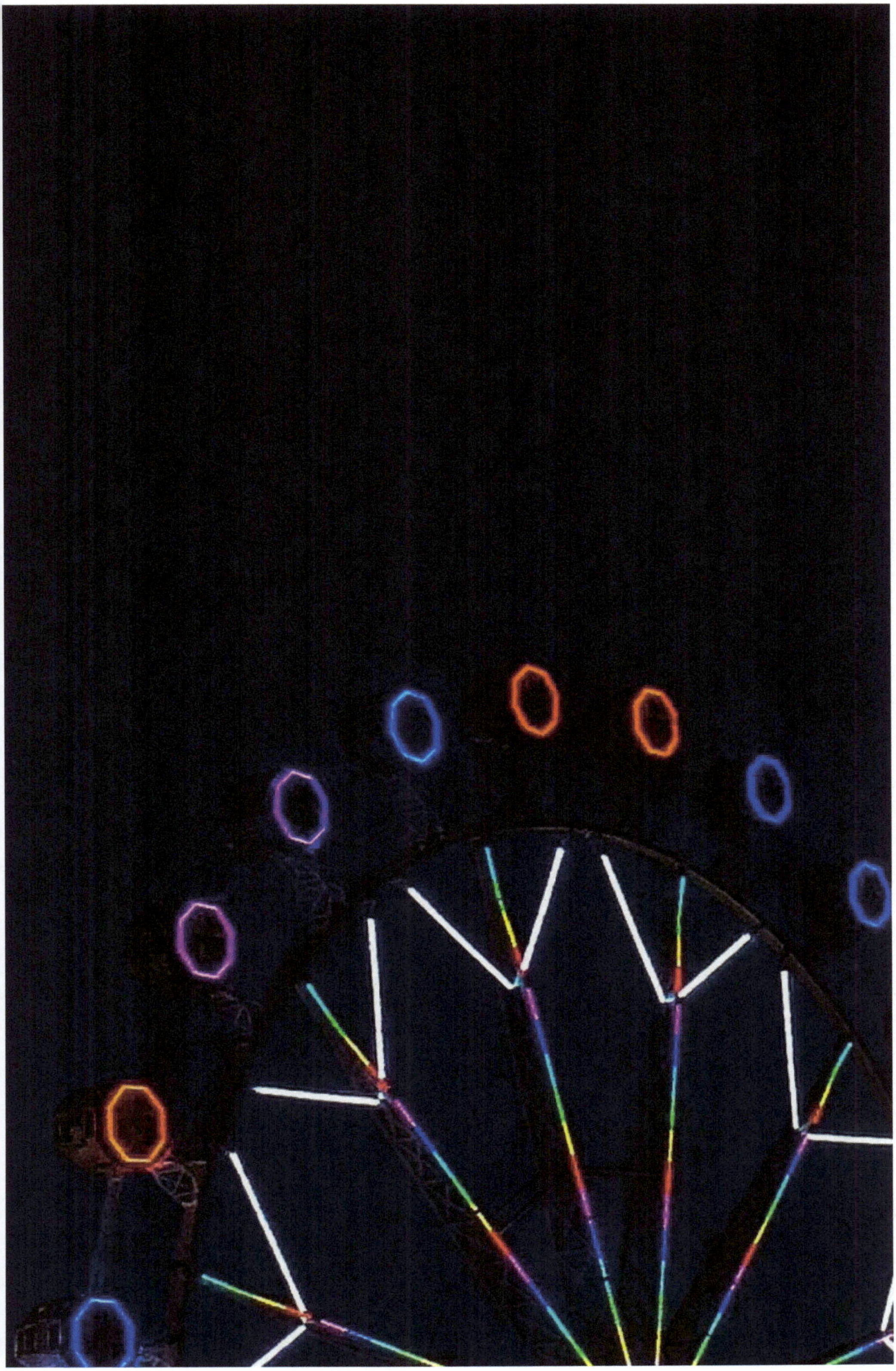

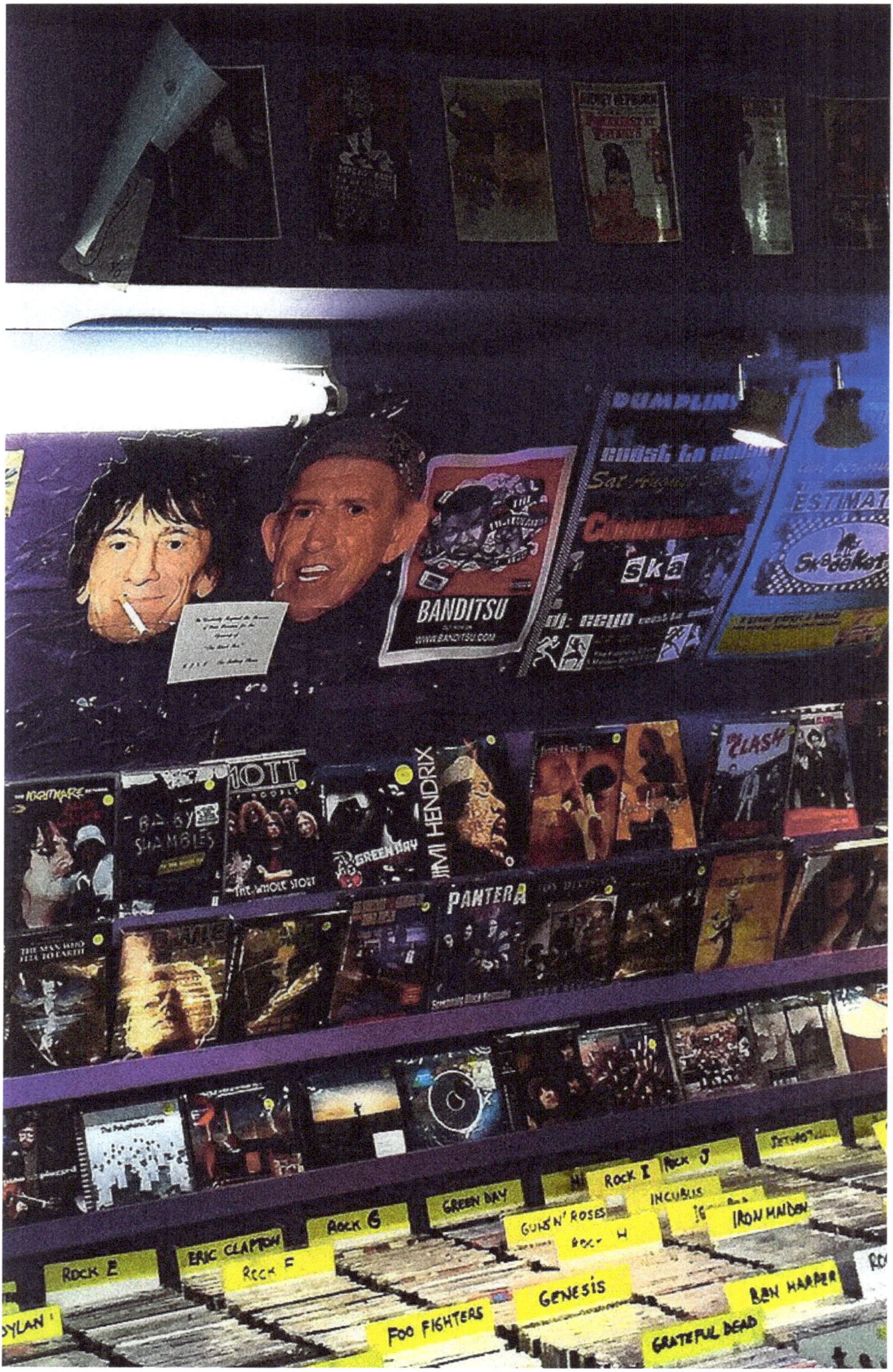
BANDITSU
WWW.BANDITSU.COM
ska
BABY SHAMBLES
THE WHOLE STORY
GREEN DAY
JIMI HENDRIX
CLASH
PANTERA
THE MAN WHO FELL TO EARTH
ROCK E
ERIC CLAPTON
ROCK F
ROCK G
GREEN DAY
ROCK I
ROCK J
INCUBUS
GUNS N' ROSES
IRON MAIDEN
GENESIS
BEN HARPER
FOO FIGHTERS
GRATEFUL DEAD

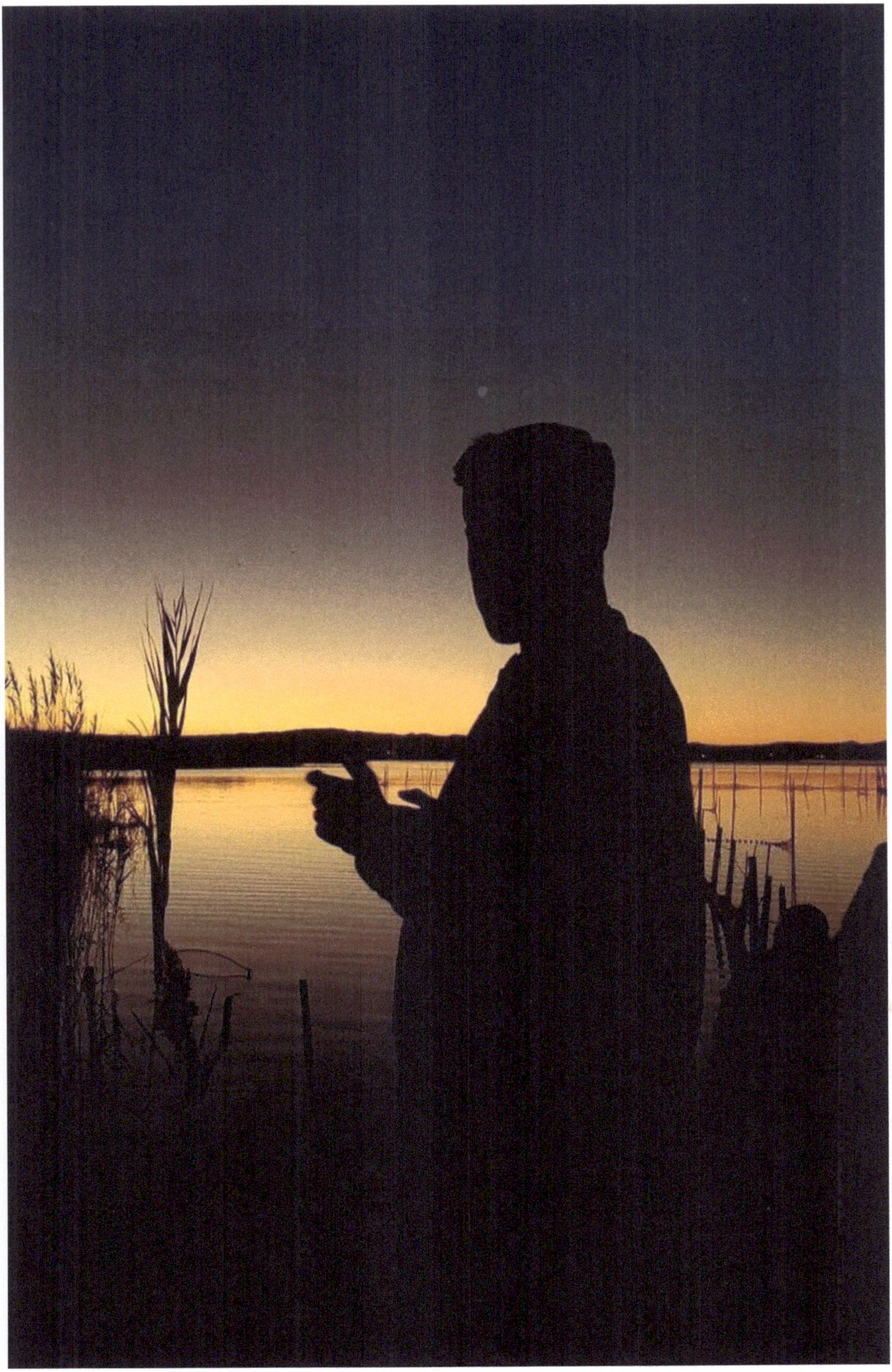

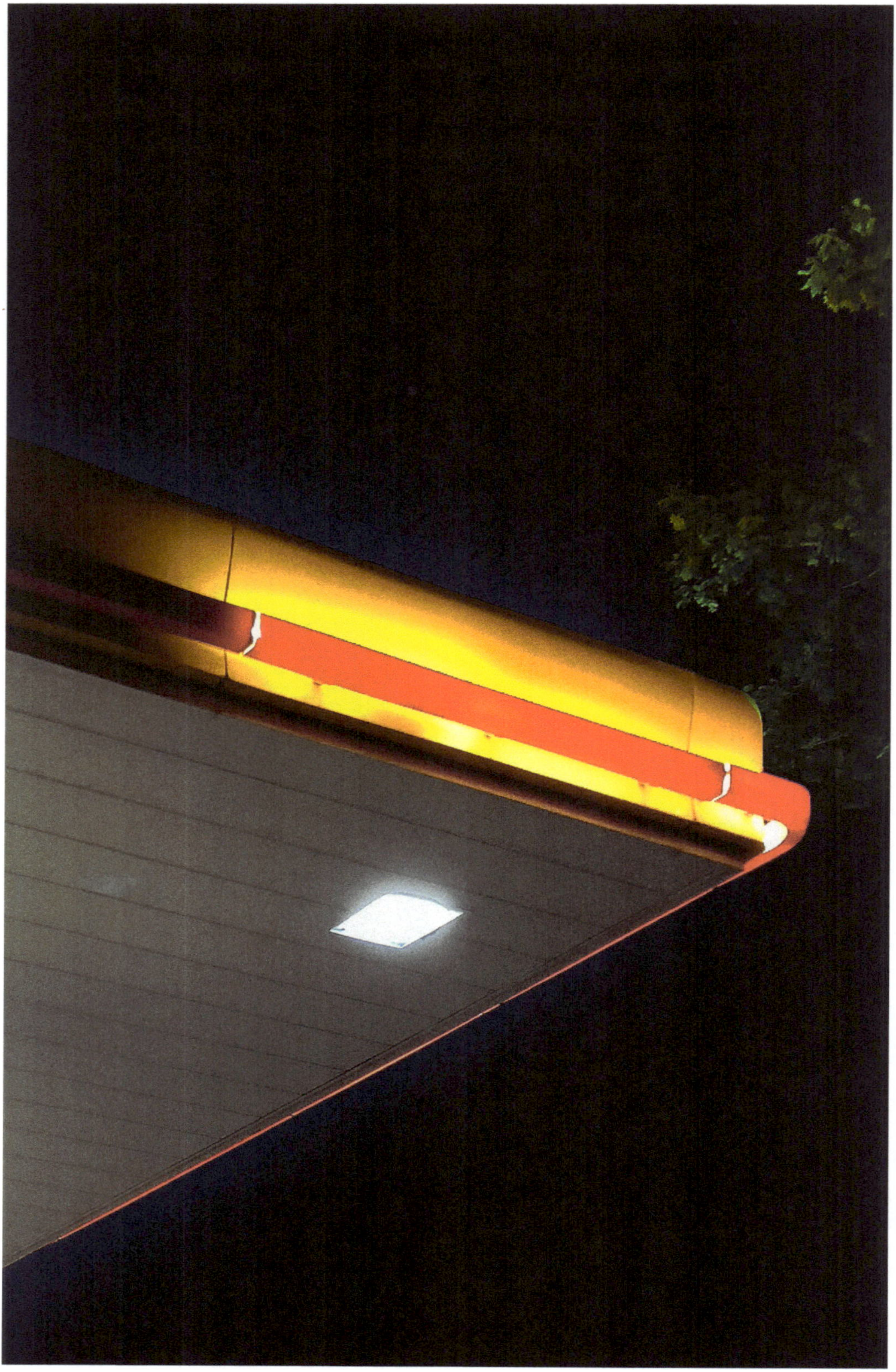

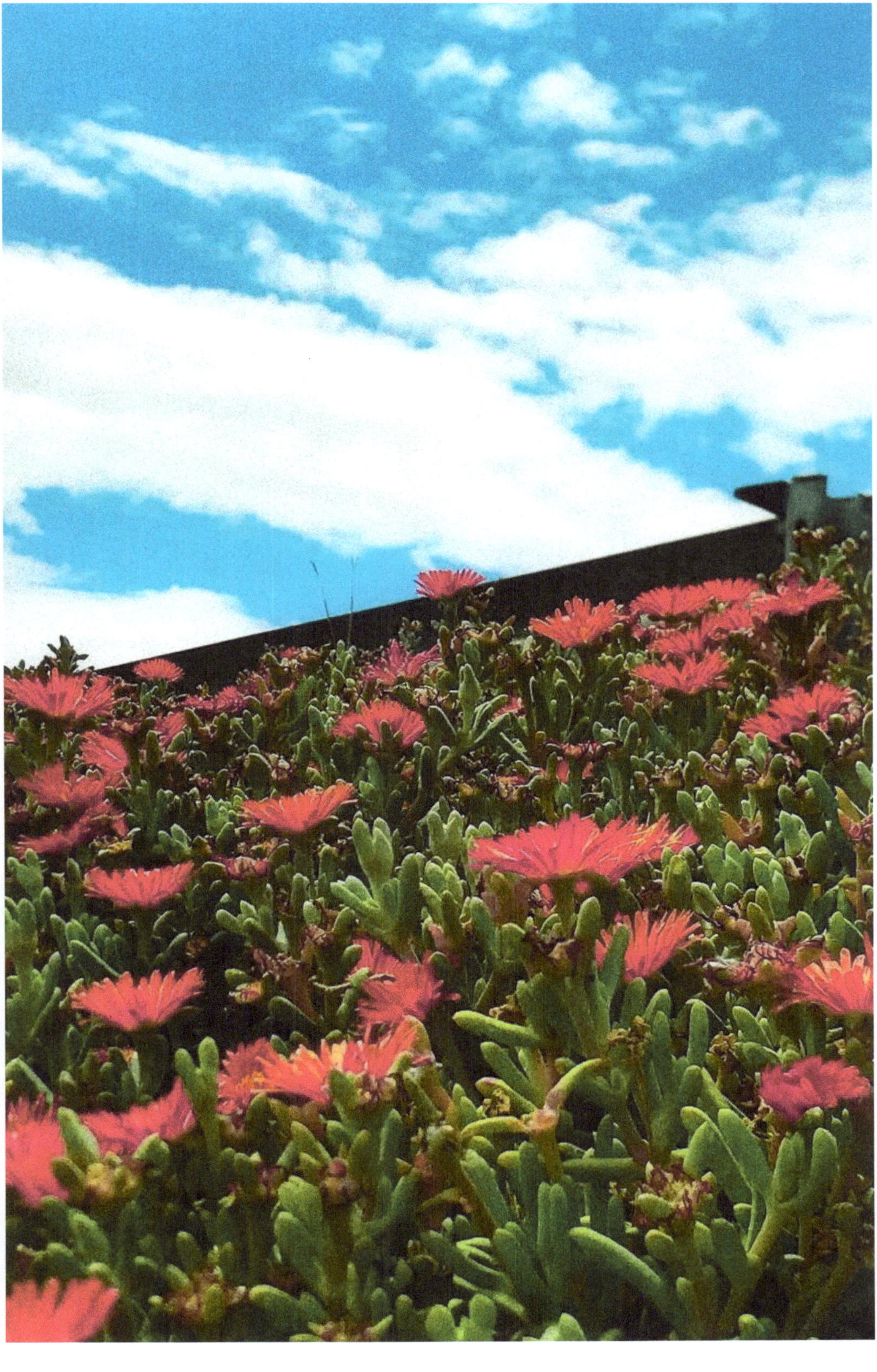

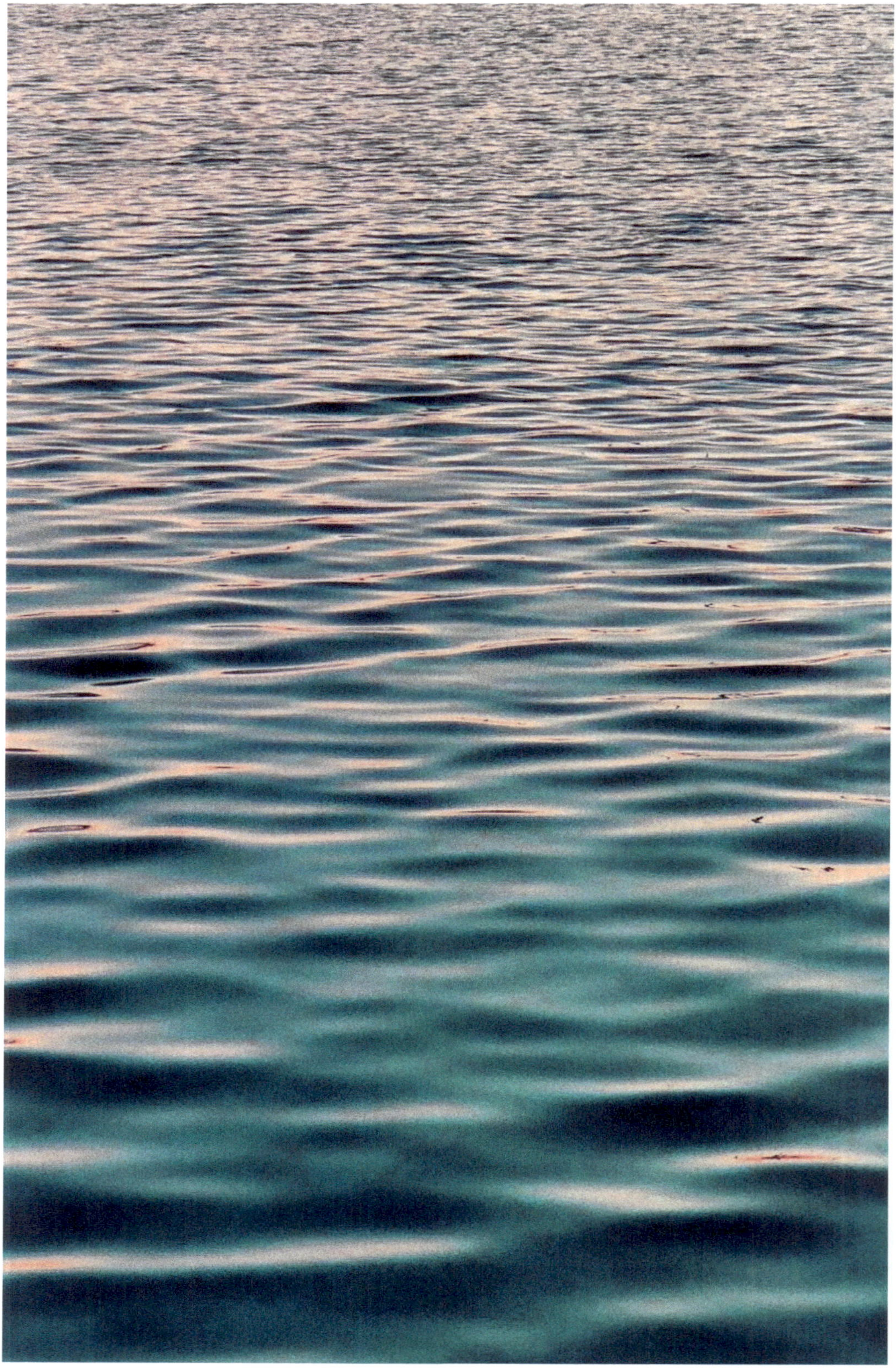

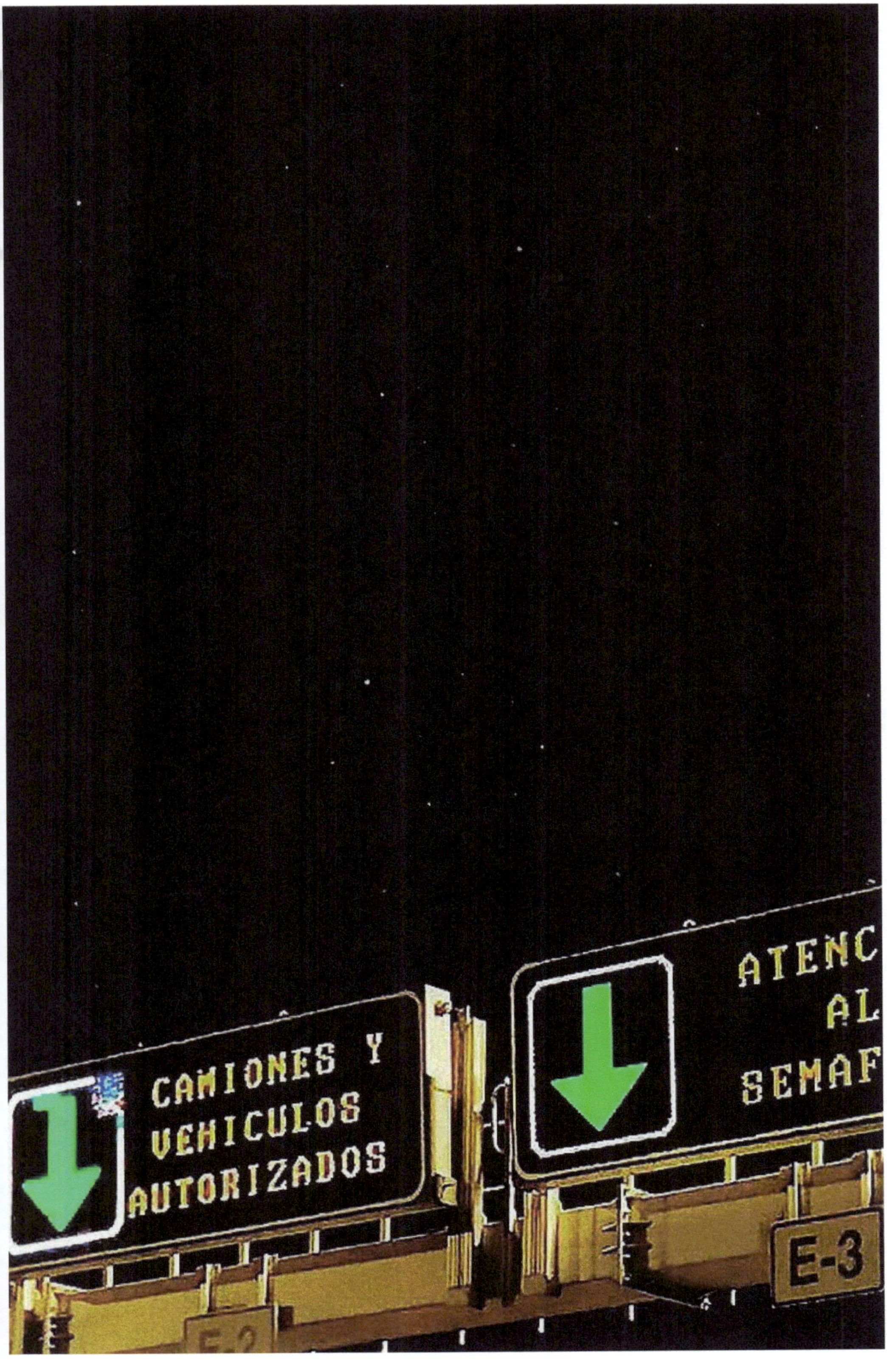
CAMIONES Y
VEHICULOS
AUTORIZADOS
E-3

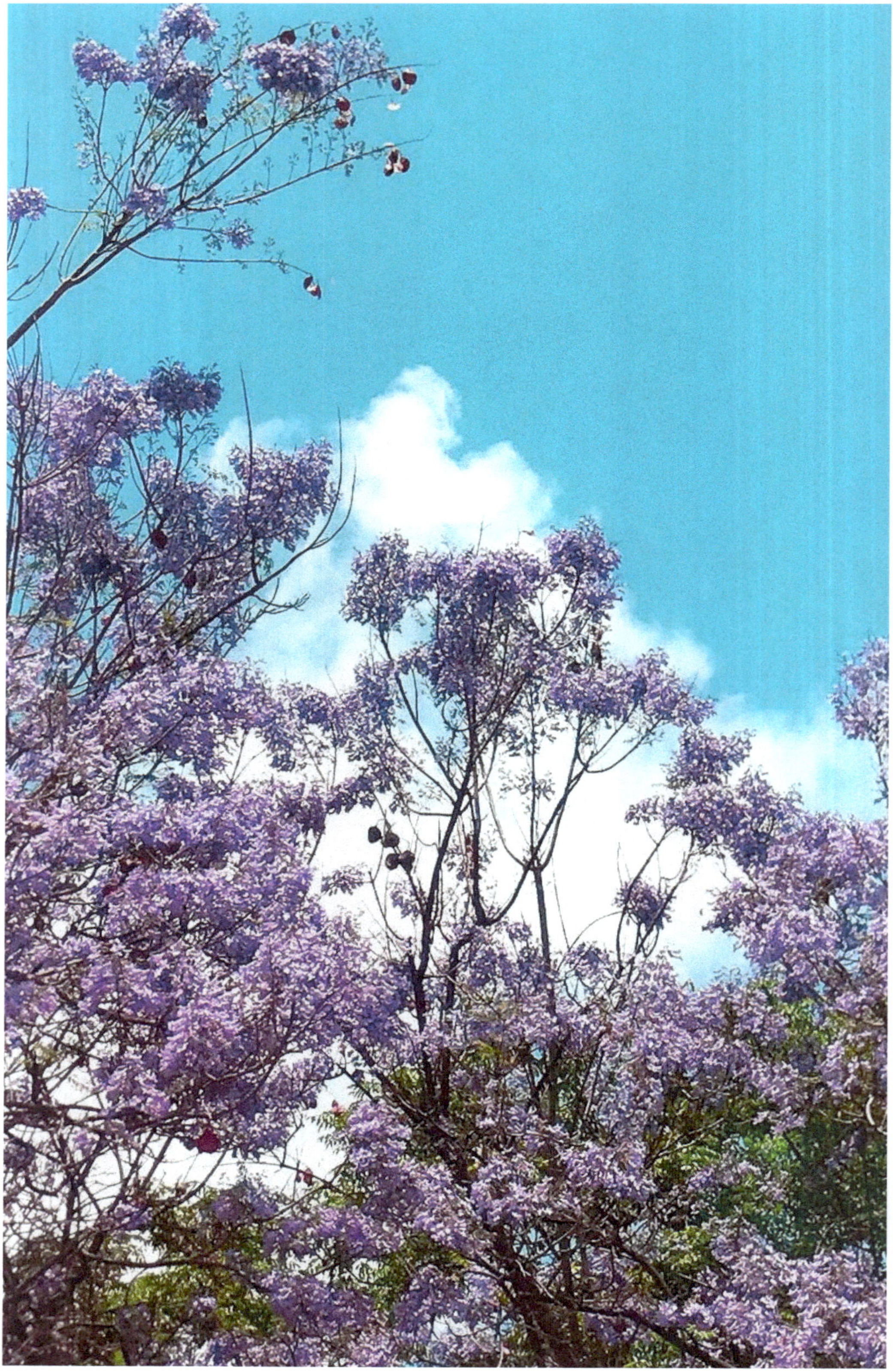

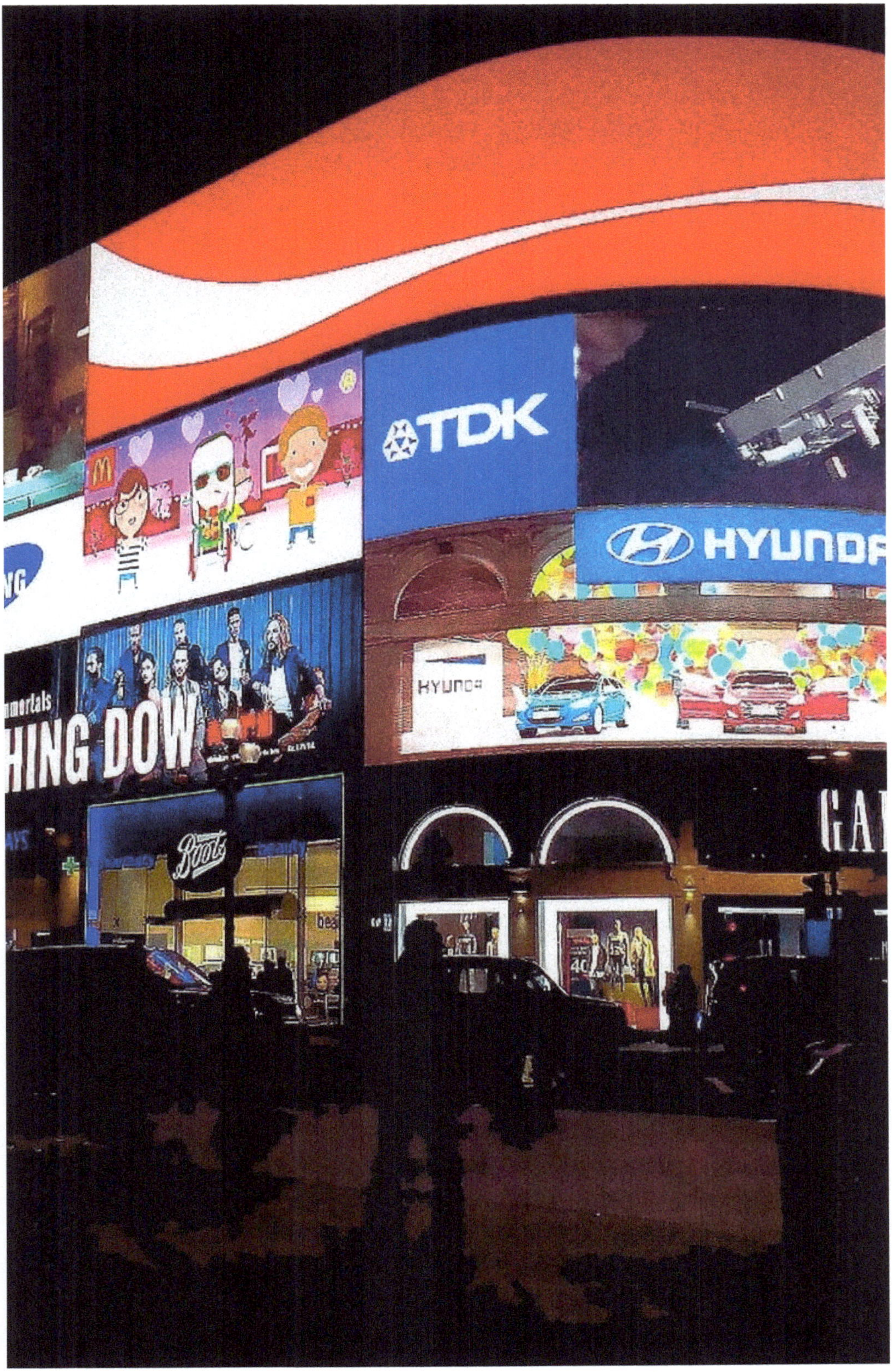
TDK
Boots

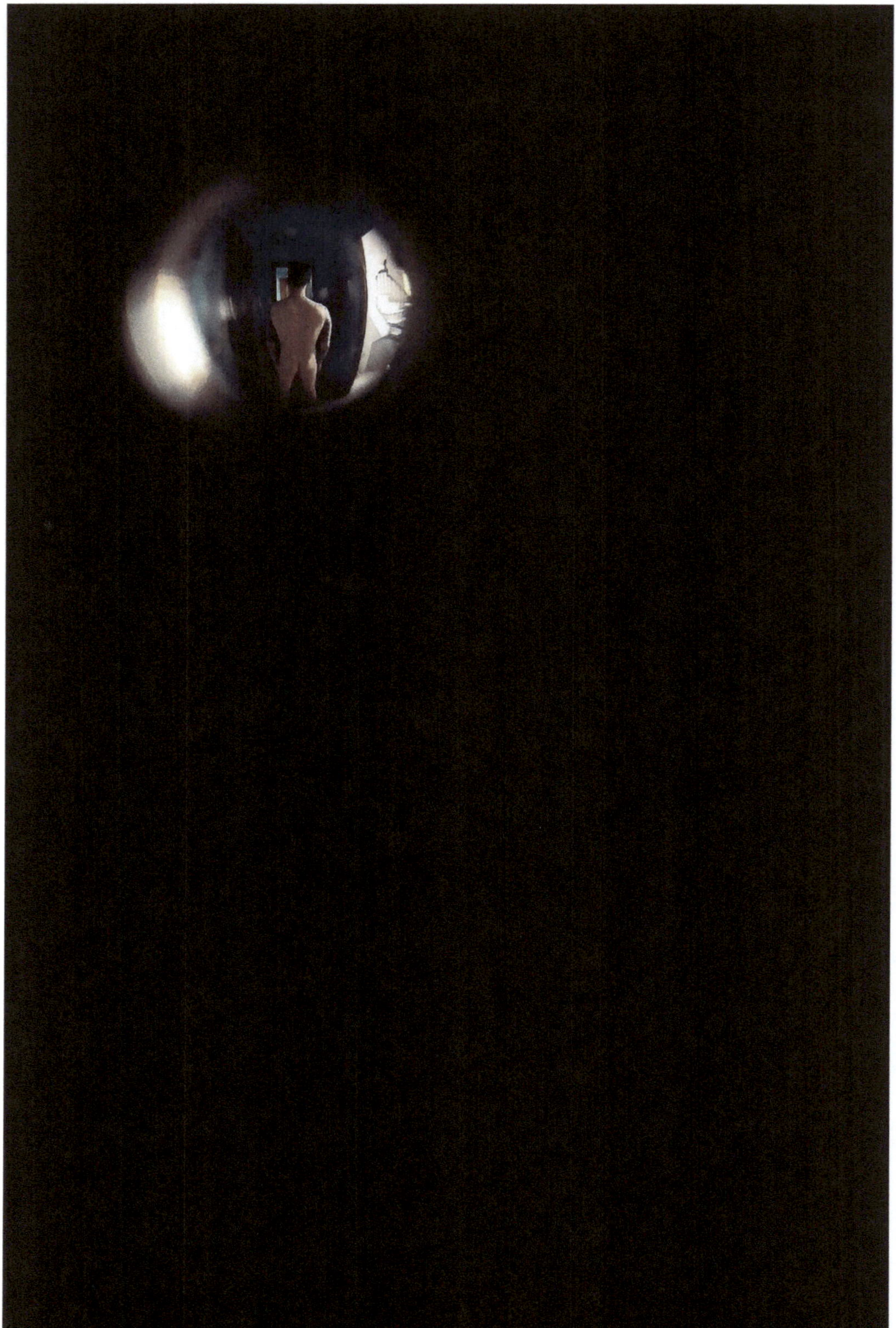

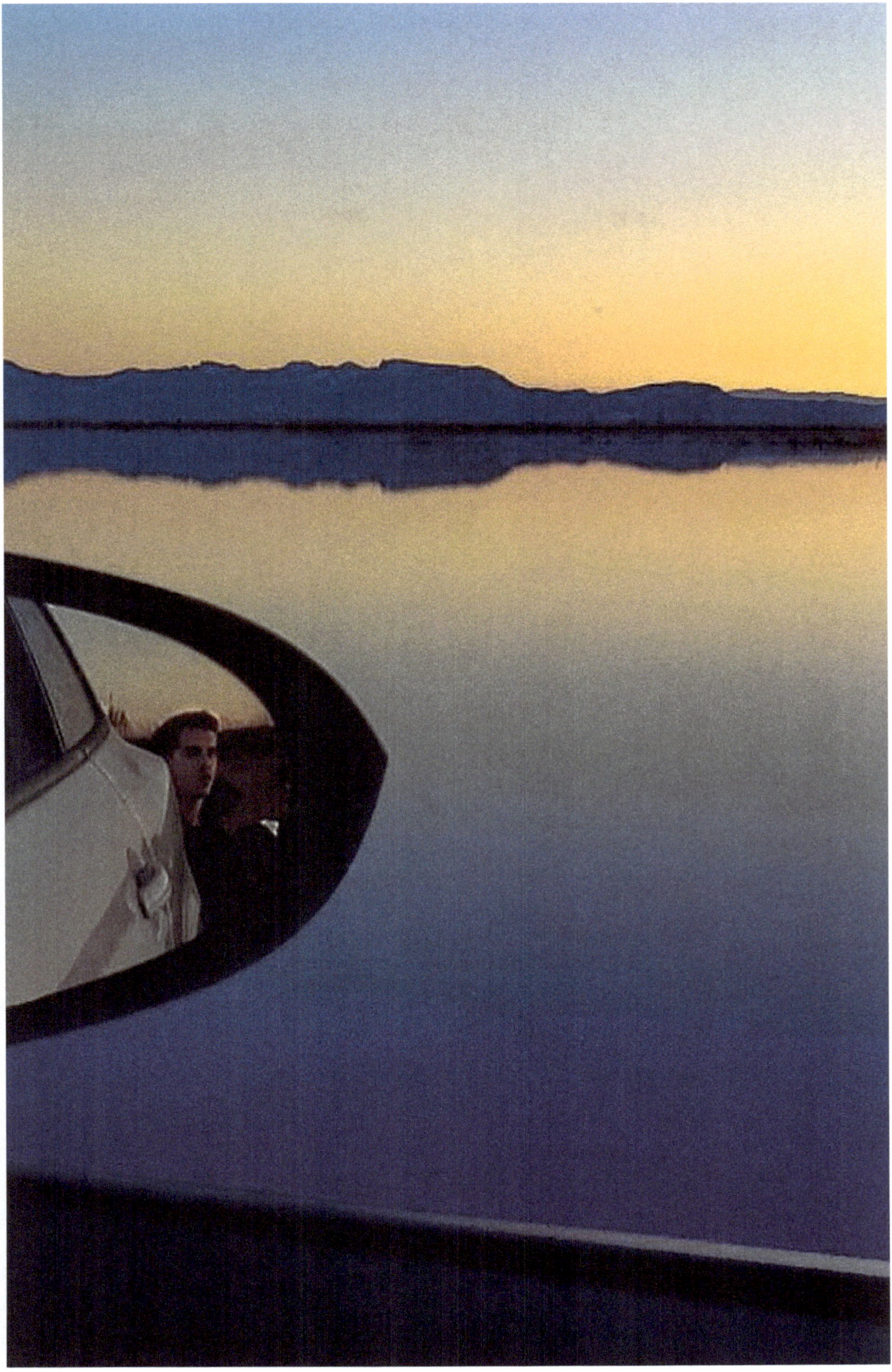

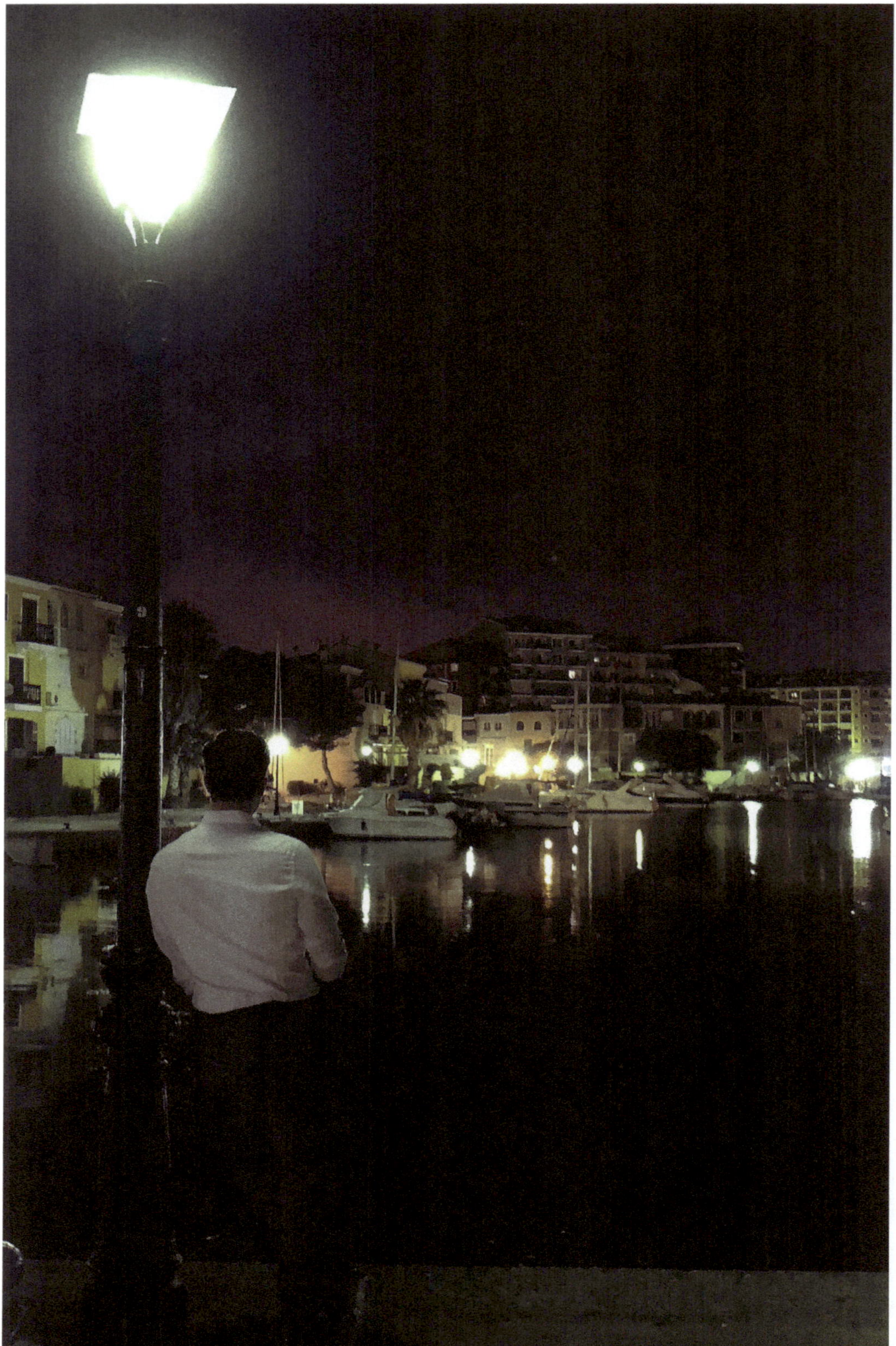

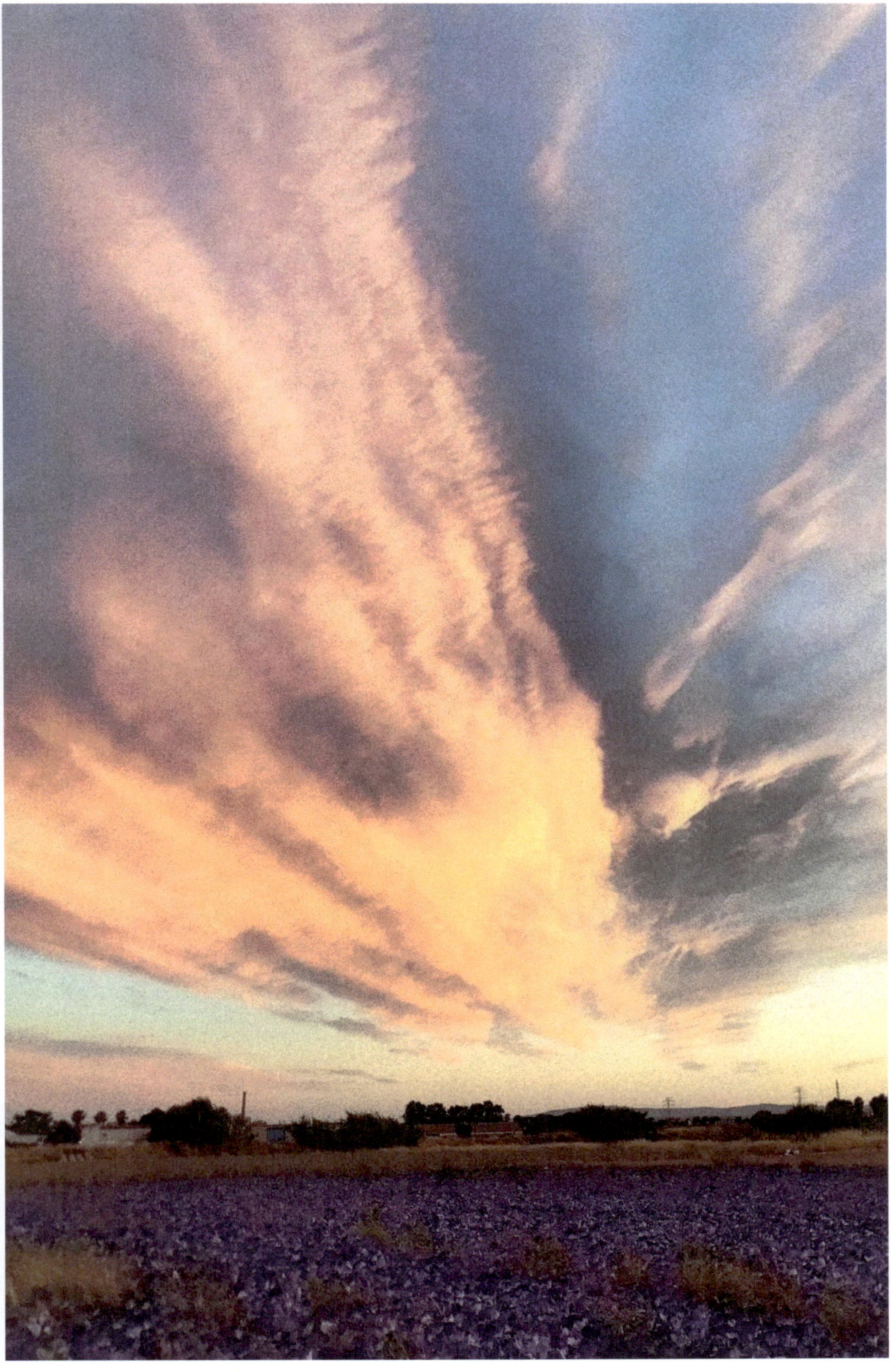

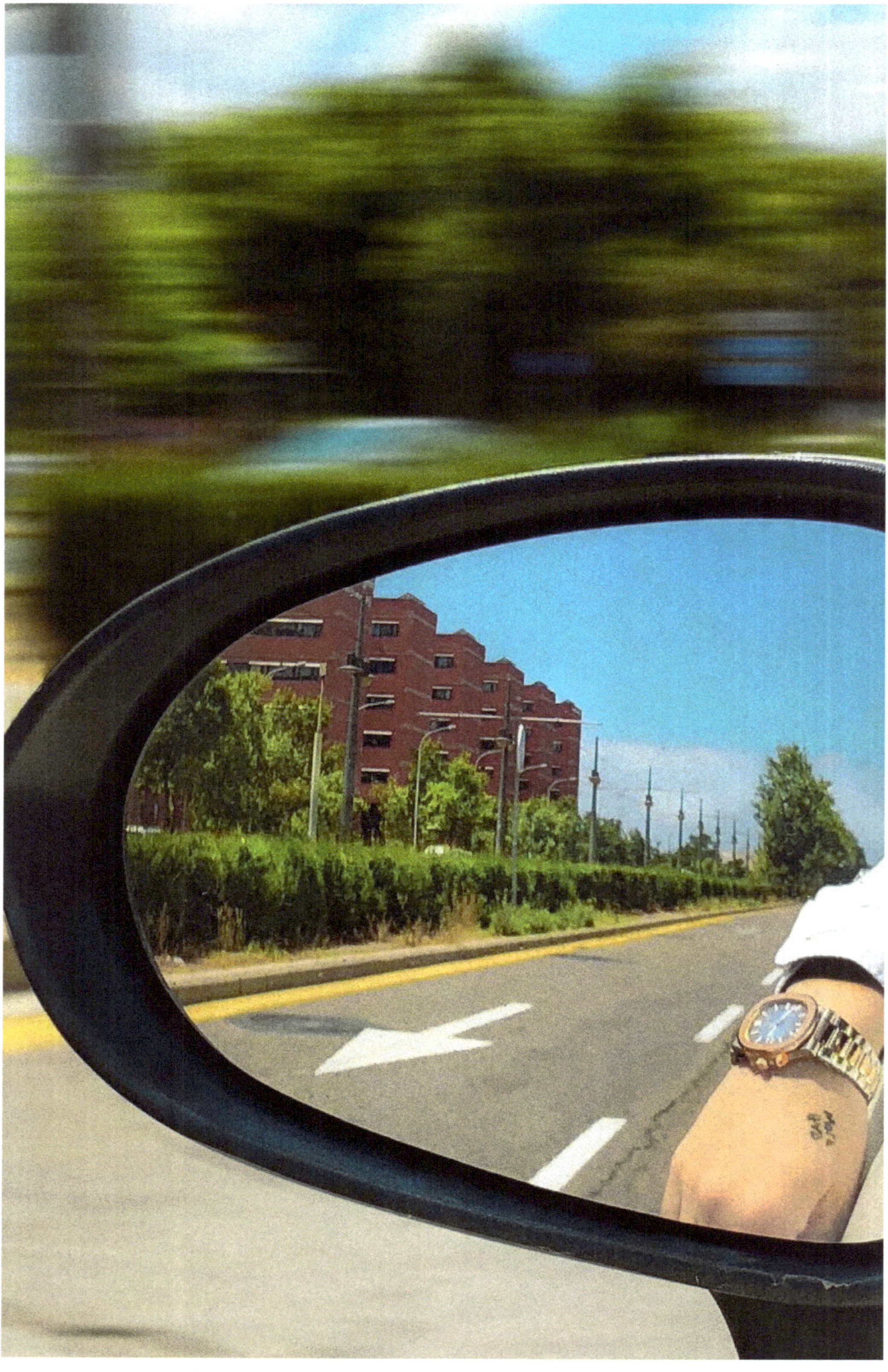

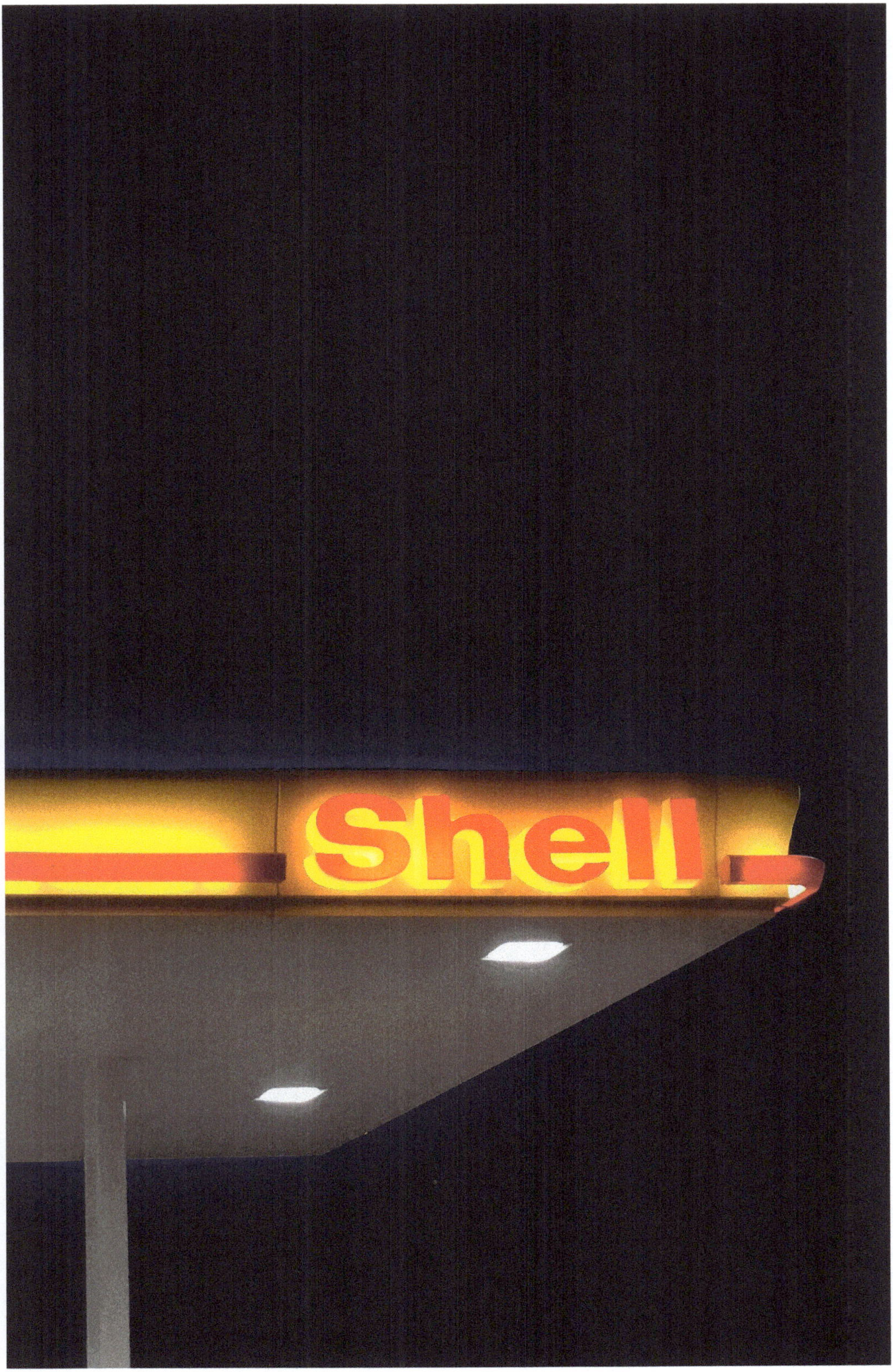
Shell

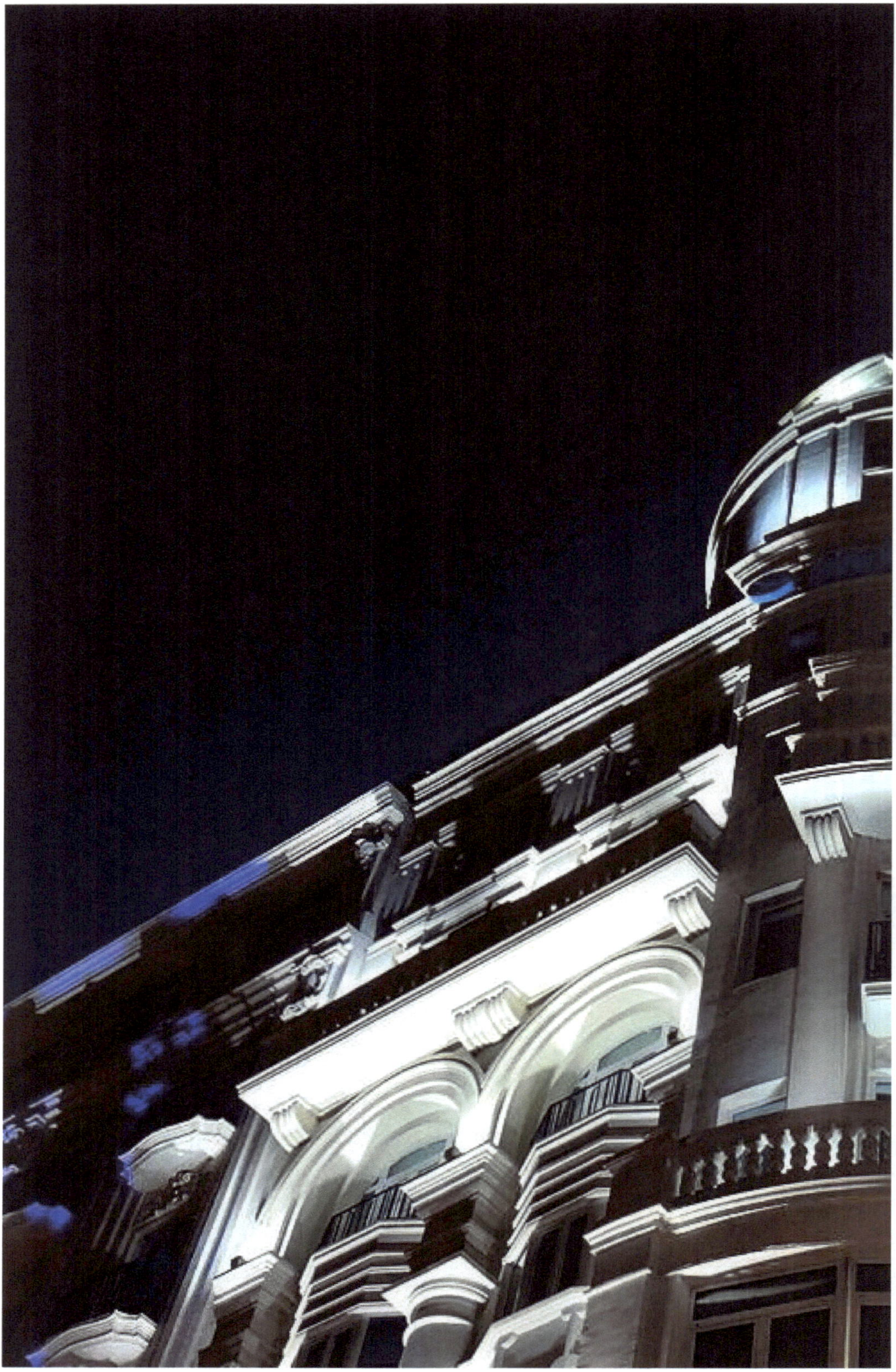

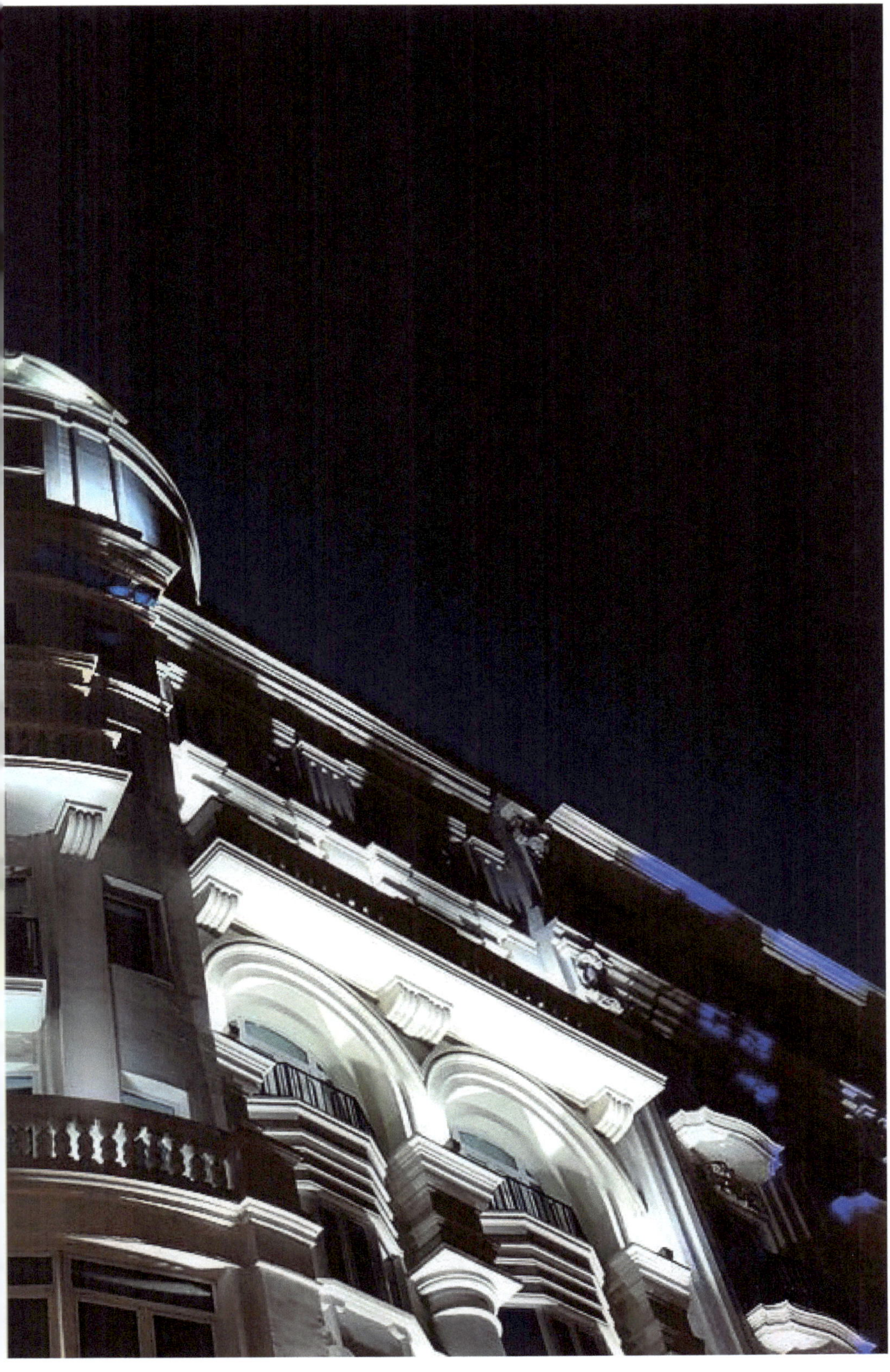

www.ingramcontent.com/pod-product-compliance
Lightning Source LLC
Chambersburg PA
CBHW040303220526
45473CB00002B/569
* 9 7 8 1 7 1 7 8 3 9 8 6 2 *